I0683397

THE
FIVE PILLARS
— · OF —
SUCCESSFUL
RELATIONSHIPS

LESTER KARPLUS

The Five Pillars of Successful Relationships
Copyright © 2024 Lester Karplus

For more information, email lesterkarplus@gmail.com.

ISBN: 979-8-89316-556-2 - ebook
ISBN: 979-8-89316-557-9 - paperback

This book is dedicated to all the people who have entered my life, especially my partner, Karna.

CONTENTS

INTRODUCTION

Like many, have you faced the complexities of relationships? Have you felt the weight of failure or the pain of betrayal? Are you fed up with unfulfilling romances? Have you ever contemplated walking away from it all? Or are you now open to exploring new perspectives and strategies for a more fulfilling relationship?

Developing meaningful relationships can be rewarding, whether you are searching for a life partner, a business ally, a trusted friend, or simply someone to share your interests with. It's a testament to the human spirit that, despite the challenges, many of us still long for the deep connections that only humans can provide.

Finding a good relationship takes time and effort. In a busy society, only some have that time. Many people spend more time finding the right job or the right home. Unfortunately, all too often, relationships start awkwardly, whether it is a lustful moment or out of convenience or dependency. The consequences are time-consuming and emotionally draining.

But there *are* successful relationships. Some last a day, while some last a lifetime. Sharing commonality and knowing why you are in the relationship is vital to a rewarding time together. This guide is for anyone wanting to start the journey toward a successful relationship. It is a philosophical approach that puts perspective on a traditional approach that may be just emotionally motivated.

I have had my share of unsuccessful relationships. Living on the planet for over seventy years and paying attention to a thing or two gets you a bit of extra wisdom that ought to be shared with the generation coming after you. Distilling and writing what I have learned took time. I have had the honor and privilege of learning from some great partners, and I dedicate this work to them.

Plenty of good books exist on healing relationships, but I need more depth and breadth to help you get started on the right foot. So, I hope this guide can help you find success in your current or new relationship.

Why Five Pillars?

Most of what has made life easier and more sensible to me has been the reduction of complex ideas into tangible and actionable advice. When I was very young, I received little help from my parents regarding relationships. The

2

frequent yelling and bickering between them left me with no desire to enter that world. My sex education was delivered in the form of a book from my father with the adage not to bother asking any questions because he probably didn't know the answers.

Fortunately, I did make some male friends, and that was amazing to me. Women friends were, however, out of reach, and despite a bit of dabbling with dating in high school, I was clueless about how men and women were supposed to relate. So, I turned inward, became a photographer in high school, and spent much time observing relationships.

Unfortunately, all my observations made for a highly complex view of relationships. The more I analyzed, the more complicated it got. Trying to understand and relate to the female sex in the 1960s was excruciatingly uncomfortable. It's much easier to take their picture and run away.

Over fifty years later, I figured out what a meaningful and functional relationship is. I have been with my wife for a couple of decades now, and we are happily married. I have many special friends I value dearly. Being in a genuine, successful, long-term relationship has made the journey worthwhile.

For every relationship I considered a "failure," I critically examined myself and the roles my partners and I played in their successes and failures. In time, it boiled down to five common elements. First, to the extent there was synergy in these three constructs:

1. Common Values
2. Common Goals
3. Common Activities

Second, each partner needed to understand the part they were to play in the relationship:

4. What do I want to give to the relationship?
5. What do I want to get from the relationship?

If your dating process can reveal the essence of the common elements and answer the two critical questions, your chances of success improve enormously. Of course, it just makes sense. But as the adage goes, "The devil is in the details."

Is It Really That Simple?

In theory, embracing the Five Pillars of a successful relationship is simple. But of course, the challenge is that the human element is as divergent in implementation as there are humans. There are barriers to getting past traumas, behavioral disorders, personality issues, ethnicity, and cultural challenges.

So, my advice for being successful is to take the Five Pillars as a framework. It is your checklist to engage a future partner to see if there is the potential to go beyond the chemistry of the moment. This work intends to help you find the commonality on a journey to a successful relationship.

I have also added tools to enhance relationship success and a review of some direction to take in case something goes wrong. This is not intended to be a handbook on fixing relationships but may provide a guide to understanding what has transpired to create a dysfunctional situation.

Lastly, to be clear, this is not a scientific study but rather a philosophical distillation of a lifetime of observations. I hope this journey into understanding your relationships provides as much reward and joy as it has for me.

WHAT IS A SUCCESSFUL RELATIONSHIP?

As humans, we survive by having relationships. From our relatives, neighbors, coworkers, friends, and significant others to the UPS driver, insurance agent, and store clerk, we navigate hundreds if not thousands of relationships. Some are incidental. Many are casual. Most are informal. We have no choice over some of our relationships, while we may avoid others.

After a while, we take many of our relationships for granted. We only think about the usefulness of the transaction we are engaged in. Did we take the time to ask how someone else is doing and stop and listen to the answer?

When we interact with another person, we often engage for a reason. We might say hello to a neighbor we barely know because we wish to be friendly to them. We ask the delivery driver how his day is going because he is a part of our lives, receiving goods from distant places. We often engage in conversations at work with our colleagues to get to know them better.

As relationships come closer to home, relationships have more connections and complexities. There may be family members we take care of. We may have children to raise. And, of course, a significant other may engage with us in many ways.

Good vs. Bad Relationships

We often hear the phrases "he/she is in a bad relationship" or "they have a good relationship." So, what do people mean by that? What defines a good or bad relationship?

We can generally agree on some apparent absolutes in good relationships: trust, good communication, shared values, and respect head up that list. However, to what degree each relationship is endowed with these attributes remains a mystery. No two relationships are the same.

Some relationships succeed despite the above attributes. Codependency, control, fear, and other dysfunctional behaviors may create the outward appearance of a good relationship, but in fact, one or both members may suffer significantly over time. When the relationship begins to erode, we begin to see it as a bad relationship.

So how do we know if we have a good relationship? First and foremost, it is functional and not dysfunctional.

Functional vs. Dysfunctional Relationships

Back in the early '70s, I had the opportunity to explore an independent study degree in community psychology. At that time in Illinois, the mental hospitals discharged all their patients to the community. My project was to create transitional employment environments for a large group referred to a local day center. I spent much time observing and trying to understand why some folks did better than others. After a couple of years on this project, I reached a phenomenal conclusion.

Most of the folks I worked with had very few relationships. And many only had relationships with other members of the same group. Interactions in the group were frequently very dysfunctional. There was an absolute correlation between the number of functional relationships a person had and their ability to have a more fulfilling life.

So, one of our projects was to enlist students from the local university to be involved in the members' lives. And sure enough, this improved the members' functionality. Predictably, someone with at least three functional relationships tended to have a more successful employment outcome than a member with less than three functional relationships. More than three relationships had little additional effect.

It is essential to emphasize the term "functional." Some members did have several dysfunctional relationships. For example, there was a middle-aged man in the group whose sister constantly yelled at him and whose other relatives shunned him because of his emotional disabilities. Once a few students from the university started visiting him every week, his dysfunctional behavior dissipated. As he met new people at his workplace, his whole life changed. This miraculous change to me was incredible. And I have seen it happen many times. Research has been done on this phenomenon. It concludes with similar results.

While functionality seems to be at the core of a good relationship, there is more to it. It is also clear that dysfunctionality is at the core of a poor relationship and will eventually cause its demise. Hence, it seems better to talk about "successful relationships."

Successful Relationships

A successful relationship is one in which both relationship members happily give and get what they want from it. Ultimately, the Five Pillars are the foundation upon which every relationship can build its Success.

COMMON VALUES

What are our values? What are our partners' values? Values are the most essential aspect of building a successful relationship. When values clash, the differences are often unreconcilable. Values are easy to say but take longer to understand, particularly when looking for commonality.

Most values are lifelong. They are often formed early in life from the influences of family, community, religion, and respected leaders. But only sometimes. For example, some people transition from one political outlook to another due to changes in life circumstances and good/bad actors in the political milieu.

Most importantly, two people forming a relationship find synchronicity in the values they hold in the highest esteem. Deciding what those values are, defining them together, and finding a common bond through them will be the bedrock of a successful partnership.

Defining Values

A value is a human belief that causes someone to act in a certain way toward others. Values cannot be defined precisely, and therein lies the challenge of determining your values while understanding the values of others.

Values can be articulated in eloquent ways. However, implementation and action speak louder. So, when ascertaining the potential for a successful relationship, time is required to observe values in action.

There needs to be a precise definition of a value. The essence of a value is the spectrum of interpretation and application of that value. Take trust, for example. Someone may be deemed trustworthy because they are money handlers for many people who always see the money get where it is supposed to go. But are they no longer reliable if they consistently show up late for appointments? There are no absolute conditions for the value of trust. Some couples may view the concept of trust in how their partner behaves with others with very different expectations. Is trust violated with overt flirting outside the relationship, or are trust violations limited to extra-relational sexual encounters?

The Gray Area of Values

The very nature of values creates a whole spectrum of nuances. And what is tolerable to one person in a relationship may not be so acceptable to another. Eric tells his wife, Susan, that she is gorgeous, and the statement is an honest assessment of her appearance. He also tells her that her hair looks great on a bad day, and they both know better. Does that mean he is a dishonest person?

Bill always returns his computers to Costco before the warranty expires and gets a new one. There is nothing wrong with the computer. He is using the dissatisfaction clause of the warranty to return it. Is this dishonest? At the same time, Bill will always give back an overpayment for a change error at the store.

Compassion has always been a strange one for me. Folks can be compassionate about their dogs to an extreme but have no hesitation to kill or eat another species. Perhaps there should be a separate value called selective compassion. Or maybe it is just speciesism…and there is no compassion.

Values are not black and white. They are shades of gray. Take honesty, for example. When your partner tells you they are working late at the office when they are having an affair, that may go off the chart in the dishonesty department. However, if they tell you traffic was bad when, in fact, they just left the office late, you probably wouldn't be concerned about the integrity of the statement.

Can you be too honest? Are opinions left unsaid dishonest? How much honesty or dishonesty can you tolerate in a friend or a partner? There is no correct answer. It is only what makes sense to you and your potential partner.

List of Values

The following list of values is presented to help you ascertain which ones are important to you. While a chapter could be written about each, the objective is to provide a thumbnail overview to stimulate your thought process. Choose the top five values most important to you. Some may seem obvious choices, while others appear more obscure:

Authenticity	Friendly	Patience
Bravery	Generosity	Perseverance
Cheerfulness	Gratitude	Political Position
Cleanliness	Helpfulness	Religiosity
Compassion	Honesty	Respect
Courage	Humility	Responsibility
Courtesy	Integrity	Reverence
Creativity	Kindness	Righteousness
Critical Thinking	Love	Spirituality
Empathy	Loyalty	Thriftiness
Fairness	Obedience	Trustworthiness
Forgiveness	Open-Mindedness	

With your top five selected, summarize what each value means to you and what you want to see in a partner. You may be surprised when you must commit to paper what you mean when you use the value. For example, patience may be an essential value to you, but then you are upset when the car in front of you takes too long to go when the light turns green. Honesty is essential, but you realize you made up an excuse for being late for a meeting.

Do not create a double standard that sets a bar higher for your partner than you can achieve yourself. Try to find shades of gray you both feel comfortable living with.

ACTION ITEM:

Select your top five values from the above list and write them down. Write a sentence for each, illustrating what makes this value important to you.

COMMON GOALS

To be in a successful partnership, both partners' goals must be aligned. Goals, however, are less immutable than values. Goals constantly change for each relationship member and may only partially align. However, they need to be reasonably aligned to have a successful relationship.

Here are some ideas for aligned goals:

- Supporting each other to complete school.

- Planning a family of similar size and time frame.
- Creating a certain amount of income or budget.
- Supporting each other's health outcomes.
- Moving to a particular location.

Examples of non-aligned goals:

- One person wants a family, while the other does not. (This could also be construed as a value, but often, people change their ideas on family goals as they age.)
- One person wants to be out of debt, while the other spends money without thought.
- One person wants to live by the ocean, while the other prefers the mountains.

List of Goals

Goals come in many shapes and sizes. They should be described as a particular outcome in a fixed period. For example, "I want us to be out of debt in twelve months." Some general goal topics:

Education	Pets
Finances	Political Achievement
Geographic Location	Projects
Health	Social Position
Housing	Sports Achievement
Kids	Travel

Goals will change as outcomes are reached. Goals may have to be negotiated or at least discussed.

Sometimes, one partner's goals will differ from those of another, which may not matter; other times, it may produce conflict. Ultimately, values come into play, and often, it is through these values that the situation is resolved. One partner may wish to be out of debt in a year, while the other must take on more debt to finish school. However, if both partners' values are aligned with the importance of a good education and frugality, the same result can be achieved in a longer time frame.

How to Check in on Goal Alignment

Together, partners choose the five most essential goal topics from the above list. Each partner writes down what they want to achieve over the next year. Then, they discuss what is possible and supportable by each other.

Irreconcilable goals should be discussed with overarching values in mind. Can a compromise be reached? Can they be achieved sequentially, with each partner taking a turn? Can they be modified, or can the time frame be changed?

ACTION ITEM:

Choose five goals you would like to achieve in the next year and two long-term goals you would like to accomplish in five years. Write them down. Use this list in discussions with potential partners or existing partners. See if your potential partner can support your goals and if you can support your partner's goals.

Once we mutually understand values and goals, we can explore the day-to-day.

COMMON ACTIVITIES

Many relationships start with the pillar of shared activities. Whether it is the outdoors, riding bikes, hiking, walking, playing golf, or sports, the opportunities to find someone who spends their time doing the same thing as you are virtually endless. And if you have more than one or two activities in common, it seems like an excellent opportunity to connect.

However, the problem with activities being the basis for a relationship is apparent. I have heard the expression that we often "age out" of an activity as we get older. At that point, our partner is also likely to age out. Is the timing appropriate for another similar activity?

I was an avid cyclist at a very young age. My first wife and I rode our bikes around the coast of Britain for a summer. She stopped riding soon after that, while I rode into my late sixties. But our focus became kids, which was the mainstay of our joint activities. And my bike riding became more practical as a bike commuter.

While values are almost immutable, goals change as you achieve them, while activities can be relatively transient. So, if your new pickleball partner is your new heartthrob, it is time to go deeper before assuming your pickleball partner is your new life partner.

Activities as a Barometer

I have observed many relationships thrive because of shared activities. If your values and goals are similar, you may gravitate to similar activities. However, while one activity in common may make a connection, the probability of a successful relationship is less likely without shared goals and values.

You both like the same movies, read the same books, buy the same stuff, and like the same food. This may be a good indicator of some synergy. However, great synergy *only* does not guarantee a great relationship. Finding the intersection and union of values and goals would be best.

Activities as an Icebreaker

A disastrous trend is happening in our society. It's called social media. For many, social media has replaced real-life activity. It is a virtual reality that allows humans to have virtual relationships behind a screen and to avoid face-to-face contact with other humans.

Choosing activities and a concerted effort to show up for them opens a world of other people who may also share your interests. Relying on similar desires or interests on social media will be far less rewarding than getting out there and doing an activity with someone.

Activities provide a window into another person's world and the potential for connection. With that connection comes the opportunity to explore goals and values. Connections indeed happen when the intersection of goals and values finds meaning.

Participating in activities is one of the best avenues to a potential relationship. Social apps may help make virtual connections. The downside to finding relationships online is there may be a disconnect when virtual life meets real life.

List of Common Activities

This list is provided to help stimulate ideas and activities you may enjoy. You may find others who participate and enjoy that same activity.

Archery	Horseback Riding
Astronomy Observation	Horse-Drawn Carriages
Beach Volleyball	Hot-Air Ballooning
Biking	Ice Skating
Birdwatching	Houseplants
Camping	Kite Flying
Canoeing or Kayaking	Knitting
Canopy Tours	LEGOs
Caving or Spelunking	Listening to Music
Concerts	Listening to Podcasts
Cooking or Baking	Meditation
Crafts	Model Building
Dancing	Nature Walks
DIY Home Improvement	Nature Photography
Drawing	Off-Roading Adventures
Eating Out	Organizing Your Space
Fishing	Orienteering
Foraging	Outdoor Cooking
Frisbee	Paddleboarding
Gardening	Painting Pictures
Geocaching	Paintball
Go-Kart Racing	Para- or Hang Gliding
Golf	Photography
Hiking	Pickleball
Home Spa Day	Picnicking

Playing Board Games

Playing Music

Puzzles

Rafting

Reading

Retreats

Rock Climbing

Rollerblading

Roller Skating

Rowing

Running or Jogging

Sailing

Sex

Skateboarding

Skiing or Snowboarding

Sled Dog Adventures

Sledding

Snowshoeing

Snuggling

Stargazing

Surfing

Swimming

Tobogganing

Tennis

Tree Climbing

Video Games

Virtual or Online Classes

Virtual Reality Games

Watching Movies/TV

Windsurfing

Working Out

Writing

Cross-Country Skiing

Yoga

Zip-Lining

Pick a few activities you think you will enjoy. For example, you could bike in the summer and cross-country ski in the winter or go to concerts and play card games.

When exploring a new relationship without everyday activities, discuss the options on the list with your potential friend to see if you can find an activity or activities in common. Of course, finding new activities to try together can enhance an existing relationship.

ACTION ITEM:

Write down five activities you like or want to do. Then, discuss your similarities and differences with your potential partner. Are there things you can do together?

By this point in the process, you have started to see a new way of looking at relationships. But now comes a critical point to explore: What do you want to give to a relationship?

WHAT DO I WANT TO GIVE TO A RELATIONSHIP?

With only a few exceptions, everyone I have asked this question answers with something like, "I never thought about it," "I don't know," or "Is that a thing?"

Paul Simon more aptly describes the modern condition in "50 Ways to Leave Your Lover." Relationships tend to end in what we are not getting and not what we are giving.

Or there is a give-to-get attitude reflected in the shallow adage "Men give love for sex, while women give sex for love." Unfortunately, this is often truer than we wish to admit.

The Grand Gives

Topping the list of Gives is probably love. By love, we could mean unrequited support, patience, understanding, kindness, loyalty, freedom, trust, acceptance, compassion, and comfort. What items do you genuinely want to give your partner in a relationship? And are these attributes of love that your partner wants to receive? Not all relationships are based on love.

The Lesser Gives

The lesser Gives often get the focus because they are more practical and easily quantified. For example, I want to share my house with a partner. The lesser Gives may include the following:

Affection	Money
Extended Family	Physical Comfort
Health Care	Shelter
Leadership	Travel Opportunity

It is essential to invoke the lesser Gives, which you are willing to give freely without expecting something in return. However, knowing what you want from a relationship is essential, so you do not feel cheated.

What If They Reject What You Want to Give?

Clarifying what you want to give is paramount to building a new relationship. If your potential partner does not like receiving what you offer, it may be time to move on.

Of course, compromise is an alternative to giving up. A lively discussion of what your potential partner wants from you and what you want from your partner is paramount to finding common ground.

It is better to discuss it now than to be in a mess a few years later because of unfulfilled expectations for both parties.

> **ACTION ITEM:**
> Write down the top three Greater Gives you would like to contribute to a relationship, followed by two Lesser Gives.

Now, let's move on to what you want to get from a relationship.

WHAT DO I WANT TO GET FROM A RELATIONSHIP?

Most people skip the question, "What do I want to get from a relationship?" This may be because much of it involves implied expectations. And in certain types of relationships, the implied expectations are apparent. We expect the server to bring us our food when we order at the restaurant. When we tutor students, we expect they will listen to our teaching.

First, Decide What You Want

You may need help deciding what you want. But at the very least, a successful long-term relationship requires two partners to give and take in harmony. And that often means you provide and take similar things from the relationship. So, that may mean that your Get list is not too different from your Give list.

Second, Discuss What You Want

Living with unspoken expectations is a great way to grind down what could have been a successful relationship. So, before jumping into that blissful union, discuss what you would like to receive. Starting that conversation may seem a bit tricky. Here are some icebreakers:

- "Can we discuss what we want to give and receive from each other in this relationship?"
- "Would you like to know what I want to give you in this relationship and what I want to get?"
- "Let's talk about our relationship, what we want to give each other, and what we want to receive."

Unfortunately, we live in a culture that is too quick to get together, and when it doesn't work out, we spend excessive time and money breaking up. Why not invest some time upfront in a positive discussion? The worst case is that you will determine you are not suited to be together because each person wants something entirely different from what their potential partner is and is not willing to provide.

Finding Common Ground

Since you and your potential partner have likely never discussed what you want from a relationship openly, Success will depend on what you both decide at the outset. While the "give and get" needs will change over time, having an open dialogue will improve the chances of *the intention* becoming a reality. If you struggle to find things your partner wants from you, return to your goals and activities lists. Discuss how you can help each other reach goals or enjoy activities more. For example, here is an exchange between Bill and Sam:

Sam: Hey, Bill, I've been thinking a lot about us lately, and I feel like we should talk about where we are and what we both want from our relationship. I want us to be clear with each other, you know?

Bill: I'm glad you brought this up. I've been thinking about it too. I care about you, and I want us to be on the same page about what we're giving and getting from this relationship.

Sam: Exactly. For me, I think the most important things I want to give are kindness, loyalty, and affection. I want to be someone you can rely on emotionally and feel safe with, and I expect the same in return. I want to know that we're in this together, that we're building something based on trust and care.

Bill: That makes sense, and I definitely feel the same about loyalty and trust. For me, I want to give you support—whether it's emotional or practical. I want to understand you and be there for you when you need someone to listen. I also want to provide some level of financial stability so we don't have to worry about that part of life too much. I feel like that's something I can contribute to our future.

Sam: I really appreciate that. I think emotional support and understanding are huge for any relationship, and having financial stability would definitely reduce stress. What do you feel like you need from me? What's important for you to receive?

Bill: Honestly, I think what I need most is a place I can call home. Somewhere I feel safe and like I belong, you know? Along with that, I want loyalty—I need to know that you've got my back, just like I'll have yours. And compassion. Sometimes, life gets tough, and I want to feel like I can come to you without judgment when I'm struggling.

Sam: I completely understand. I want you to feel like you have that safe place with me. Compassion is something I value a lot, too. I think we're on the same wavelength. If we both focus on being kind, loyal, and supportive, I think we can build something really strong.

Bill: I agree. I feel good knowing we both want to invest in each other emotionally and practically. It's nice to know we're both thinking long-term and willing to give and receive what matters most to us.

Sam: It's good to know we're on the same page. Let's keep communicating like this so we don't lose sight of what we both need and want.

Bill: Definitely. Communication is vital, and I'm all in. We've got this.

ACTION ITEM:

Similar to the Gives, write down the top three Greater Gets you would like to contribute to a relationship, followed by two Lesser Gets.

TWO HALVES DON'T MAKE A WHOLE

Over the last couple of generations, a frequent phrase has been used to refer to a partner or spouse as your "other half" or "better half." Tongue in cheek implies that two people together somehow make a whole. Also, it means we are only complete if we have a partner.

Finding a partner who can compensate for our deficiencies may be an excellent way to improve our relationship. You can have all the bases covered. Indeed, this is a pragmatic approach. However, unless the common goals, values, and activities are lined up, the prognosis of Success is low.

More importantly, however, two halves are often born from an individual who cannot do life properly alone. This, in turn, drives them to find a partner to help them. This leads to interesting dynamics if the deficiencies are emotional or intellectual. How long will the caretaker endure? Will the dysfunctional dynamics become functional because each person accepts their role?

So, the bottom line is that every human must ensure they can care for themselves before caring for someone else if a successful relationship is to be the outcome.

Self-Actualization

Abraham Maslow first introduced the concept of self-actualization in 1943. People are self-actualized if they realize their full potential and purpose in life. They are motivated by creativity, autonomy, authenticity, and a sense of connection to something greater than themselves. He estimated that only 1 percent of the population achieved a state of self-actualization. The self-actualized person is genuinely the whole person.

If this is true, we are all doomed to create unsuccessful relationships. But in fact, it is all relative. Hopefully, everyone is on a journey to self-realization and self-actualization. So, working on yourself as much as on the relationship ensures optimized Success.

ARRANGING YOUR MARRIAGE

Arranged marriages were customary for many centuries worldwide and only began to diminish in the last couple of generations. Today's arranged marriages have more say from the participants, so they are not too indifferent from a planned autonomous marriage.

Arranged marriages have many benefits, especially when the parents consider the long-term well-being of their sons or daughters. Sometimes, even a matchmaker may make a better choice than a young person who may be jaded by impractical choices and clouded by infatuation.

However, current research finds that the outcomes of successful relationships are not consistently influenced by whether the marriage is arranged or not. This may be due to the participants' greater involvement in arranged marriages.

The exciting point about arranged vs. free-choice marriages is that whether you marry for love or because it has been arranged does not produce a preferential factor to Success. Perhaps, intrinsically, each participant's shared values, goals, and activities are known well enough to the arrangers to create a sound basis for a relationship. Love can come later.

Because arranged marriages use objective and subjective approaches to help create successful relationships, we can draw parallels to free-choice marriages. Applying the Five Pillars to building a relationship may have the same outcome as an arranged marriage. Adding the components of love and romance may double our chances of Success.

So, then, is love an essential component of a successful relationship?

WHAT'S LOVE GOT TO DO WITH IT?

The Hollywood notion of marriage is to fall in love, get married, and live happily ever after. Far from that, however, more than half of all first marriages end in divorce within eight years. And even more alarming is that second and third marriages are even shorter.

So, if love is the basis for most marriages today and Success is a 50/50 probability, why do so many people get married? Is it cultural norms? Between Hollywood, Madison Avenue advertising, and the industry built around getting married, cultural expectations are set up to fail. Perhaps marriage is becoming a commercial institution.

For many, romance feels like magic. Some might call it chemistry. And who wouldn't want to keep that feeling? So, it may seem like marriage should follow to preserve that magical feeling. However, marriage rates have fallen almost 60 percent in the last fifty years. Perhaps that will change with Gen Z, most of whom desire to get married. Whether or not this Success is driven by economic necessity, government incentives, or changing values remains to be seen.

What is love? We all have notions of it. We all experience it in some way. But it has an entire spectrum of definitions and nuances. The Greek philosophers defined seven types of love. Similarly, psychologists and philosophers often define it with four, six, seven, or eight types. I will argue for six kinds of love with my philosopher hat on. They are all on a spectrum from self-centered to selfless. While a relationship may have a predominant type of love, the more that all kinds are at play, the more likely it is a healthier relationship.

- Self-Love
- Passionate or Romantic
- Unrequited
- Practical
- Compassionate

- Selfless

One issue that should be addressed here is that there is a functional, healthy version of each of these loves and a dysfunctional, unhealthy version. Understanding what you want to give and get in a relationship and your partner's motivations (relating to each functional form of love that works for both parties) is crucial for that relationship's success.

Self-Love

Without self-love, the probability of having a functional relationship with another person is slim. Self-love can take on many forms, from emotional well-being to mindfulness. But it can be equally damaging when manifested through selfishness.

The fundamental components of self-love include the following:

- Self-Acceptance
- Self-Awareness
- Self-Care
- Self-Compassion
- Self-Confidence
- Self-Empowered
- Self-Gratitude
- Self-Respect
- Mindfulness
- Personal Development

If you can comfortably say you can check off most of the list above, you have the self-love to make a relationship work. The flip side is selfish behavior. Here are some of these characteristics:

- Self-Entitlement
- Self-Gratification
- Self-Preoccupation
- Using others to get what you want
- Not relating to others' feelings
- Inability to receive feedback

If you honestly examine these characteristics and have a propensity for several, it's time to examine yourself closely. Are you ready to share life with someone else?

Passionate or Romantic Love

Passionate or romantic love is emphasized over all else in Western culture. And while it can lead to a successful relationship, it can also be the relationship's demise. If combined with the Five Pillars, Success is far more likely. Some of the benefits of passionate love include the following:

- Enhancement of relationship-positive factors
- Physical and emotional intimacy
- Sense of belonging

However, a relationship based purely on passion without regard to the connections between the Five Pillars has a downside. Here are some of the flags:

- Communication breakdown
- Conflict
- Dependency
- External stresses
- Jealousy
- Loss of passion by one partner

Unrequited, Obsessive, and Codependent Love

It is sad, but often the case, it is a relationship built on a one-sided view. The most obvious one is unrequited love. This is evident when an individual loves someone, but the person they love does not love them back. And this, in reality, is a non-relationship. Or, in some cases, a semi-relationship. The non-participant may take advantage of the party who is showering affection, giving material gifts, and giving compliments. Some pillars may hold up this kind of relationship, but in the end, it will be dysfunctional.

Obsessive love also falls into a similar category. However, in an obsessive relationship, the party who is the object of the obsession may be a willing partner. This will likely lead to dysfunctional behavior.

One of the most common dysfunctional love categories is codependent behavior. Codependent behavior occurs when one or both partners in the relationship sacrifice personal happiness to please their partner. On the outside, looking in, a codependent partner may appear loving and caring, but internally, they are sacrificing what they genuinely want in order to please their partner. Often, this can be the result of growing up in similarly dysfunctional families where codependency is the norm.

Sarah and Mark have been together for five years. Sarah is deeply empathetic, always wanting to help others, while Mark has struggled with confidence and anxiety for most of his life. Early in their relationship, Sarah found it fulfilling to support Mark emotionally, encouraging him through his bad days, listening to his problems, and reassuring him constantly. Mark felt secure in Sarah's care, relying on her to manage his feelings.

Over time, however, the dynamic shifted. Mark began to lean heavily on Sarah for validation in all aspects of his life, from work decisions to his mood. Sarah would drop everything if Mark had a bad day to help him feel better. She became his emotional crutch, and over time, she stopped focusing on her own needs and desires. Her hobbies, friendships, and career took a back seat as she centered her energy around keeping Mark happy and stable.

Despite the emotional toll on Sarah, she convinced herself that Mark's well-being was her responsibility. She felt that if she didn't step in to "save" him, he would fall apart, and it would be her fault. When Sarah expressed feeling drained or exhausted, Mark would become upset, feeling abandoned or guilty, which made Sarah quickly suppress her feelings to avoid conflict.

This cycle marked their relationship: Mark's dependency on Sarah grew while Sarah's sense of self diminished. Neither felt truly happy, but both believed they couldn't function properly without each other. Mark feared being alone, and Sarah believed her worth came from "fixing" fixing" fixing" fixing" Mark.

This unhealthy dynamic—where one partner relies heavily on the other for emotional support and the other sacrifices their needs to maintain the relationship—reflects classic codependency. Over time, it became clear that both Sarah and Mark needed to address their emotional health individually in order to build a healthier, more balanced relationship.

Once both parties realize the codependency in a relationship, it can be reversed if they are willing to work toward interdependence. This means both parties agree on mutually beneficial behaviors and treatments. At this point, the Five Pillars can enter the relationship.

Practical Love

We see practical love in arranged marriages, political marriages, and marriages of convenience. No romance is involved in the start of these relationships (though that may evolve). Practical love may be the most useful application of the Five Pillars to help project a sense of longevity.

Compassionate Love

From a positive perspective, compassion in a relationship is very beneficial. Compassion is commonly viewed as the ability to sense and then relieve the physical, emotional, or mental pain of others. If both members of a relationship contribute compassion, the relationship is enhanced. However, if one plays the victim, counting on their partner's good nature and compassion, the relationship becomes codependent and thus dysfunctional.

We also must be careful what we do with compassion. Is the burden we relieve for someone else a help to them? Or is the act of perceived kindness something we do to feel good about ourselves?

Selfless Love

Selfless, or unconditional love, is an act of love in which one gives to another without expecting anything in return. It is often considered the highest form of love, enhancing both parties.

However, selfless love can also be confused with unrequited love. And, of course, if someone expects a response from a partner, it is no longer selfless love but unrequited love.

When We Say "I Love You"

When we say "I love you," what are we saying? Does it mean you love that person's appearance or how they act? Is it the desire to have sex with them? Or is it a catchall phrase that means you care about them, want to spend time with them, or like something specific about them?

So, the next time you hear that phrase spoken to you or use it yourself, it may be time to get specific.

A GOOD GUT FEELING

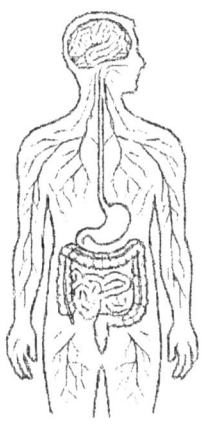

Some folks choose to pursue a relationship based on gut feelings. Depending on the quality of the "gut intelligence," this could be a successful or failed enterprise. Much of what we have presented is a very intellectual approach to relationships. Why? Because the focus of most relationships often lacks thought or is made with an unhealthy gut.

What Is a Gut Feeling?

The connection between the gut and the brain, often called the gut-brain axis, significantly influences emotions and mental states. This bidirectional communication system involves the central nervous system, the enteric nervous system, and the gut microbiota. Some of the key emotions and mental states influenced by the gut-brain connection are anxiety, depression, stress, emotional well-being, fear, and resilience.

In addition, emerging research indicates that the gut-brain axis can also affect cognitive functions such as learning and memory. So, not only can the gut create emotional distress, but it can also impair cognitive function.

Nearly 40 percent of the US population suffers from gut health issues. Given the widespread use of antibiotics, this may be significantly understated. Can you trust your gut to make a good decision?

Reconciling Gut Feelings

The odds are against gut feelings being the best guide for Success. We, therefore, must use our intellectual capacity and apply the Five Pillars process to help us make the best relationship decisions.

Of course, paying attention to your gut feelings is still important. This is especially true for healthy people who trust their gut and its outcomes.

Balancing the brain intelligence with that of the gut will improve your Success.

INTENTIONS OR EXPECTATIONS?

I couldn't, in good faith, write this book without introducing the concept of intentional living rather than living with expectations. It has been a guiding force for me for the last few decades, and I will assert it changes everything in your life, including relationships.

We live in a very self-centric culture. We expect a lot, and expectations heavily drive us. We expect a specific result: package delivery, health outcomes from drugs or surgery, smooth traffic, working internet, or people attending a scheduled meeting.

Rather than expecting an outcome, how about manifesting an outcome? Manifestation of an outcome occurs when we focus on our desires, thoughts, and intentions.

Intentions shift our thinking. Instead of attachment to the outcome, we are intimately part of making things happen. And though I hesitate to put this out there, intentions have a magical effect on a journey not bound by expectations.

Intention is willing yourself to behave in a certain way. So, when you order a package from Amazon, you engage in a process you realize may not be on time, may be the wrong item, or may not arrive at all. It is not expected to come tomorrow, even though that's what the website says. When you receive the package two days later, and it is the wrong item, you know it was part of the journey you engaged in, and eventually, the correct item is found, and you have completed the transaction. The transaction is a journey you engage in while committing to behaviors that help you complete it successfully. If you engage in the transaction with the expectation that the package will arrive tomorrow and it does not, you will be frustrated because the expectation wasn't met.

I learned about intention late in life. My partner at the time and I had just decided to end a long-term relationship as we headed down different paths in our lives. I moved out and had to find a place to live. I was having no luck when a friend mentioned a woman who traveled extensively, didn't have a home, but always seemed to land a place to live whenever she needed it. I contacted her and invited her for coffee to tell me how to create this magic.

It was an exciting conversation that created a massive shift in my whole attitude about life. To manifest anything, she told me, is to set intention. So, in reality, houses didn't just pop up for her. She was always in the process of finding housing. But not necessarily consciously. She mentioned her needs to all her friends, checked all the housing ads online regularly, and built a network of people in the business. Whenever she was in the market, she let everyone know. Someone always knew of something in short order.

The key to her Success was having no rigid expectations. She had a rough budget but often got house-sitting jobs. That meant she saved enough money on rent to afford more if a house-sitting job was unavailable. She had some minimum standards and location constraints, but they were loose enough to prevent a failure.

This seemed impossible. I went home and pictured where I wanted to stay for a while. The image of a cabin on the river came to my head. So I started looking into every source I could think of and told all my friends. A few days later, I was amazed when I found a house for rent in Boulder Creek. Part of my Success came from setting an intention and then manifesting my energy toward that intention. I have never stopped doing that; with little exception, I have manifested everything I wanted.

What became clear to me in this process is that the intention-to-manifestation process has a couple of essential rules. First, the manifestation never occurs in your precise time frame. Second, it is always slightly different from what you intended. Sometimes, it is beyond your wildest imagination.

Applying Intention to Your Relationships

One of the most significant cultural divides in relationships is expectations. Once a partner fails to fulfill expectations enough times, a breakdown occurs. Trust then becomes the false flag of unfulfilled expectations. In other words, I may think I can't trust this person after being often disappointed by unfulfilled expectations. However, in reality, my expectations are letting me down, not issues of trust.

I will even guess that most communication breakdowns in relationships are an extension of unfulfilled expectations. John tells Sally he's going to the store to get a few things for dinner. Sally is upset when John comes home without her favorite ice cream. John is initially caught off guard when he hears this. Because she did not say anything, John expected to only shop for dinner. Sally expected that John would know there was no more ice cream in the freezer. The unfulfilled expectations led to an argument.

If John and Sally applied intentions to this interaction, there would be more communication up front. John would share his intentions for dinner, and Sally would share her intentions for dessert. Without expecting an outcome, they would work out a direction they both like and would enjoy the manifestation's outcome.

The distinction in approach is subtle, but once it is shifted, you will be surprised at how much better a relationship can be. Share your values, goals, and activities with intention and manifest what you both want together.

Applying Intentions When Starting Over

Armed with intentional living and the Five Pillars, you could hardly fail if you are starting over.

Begin by analyzing past relationships and your successes and failures. Then, analyze them relative to the Five Pillars and see how you could have planned better. Decide if you are ready for a new relationship.

Write down what you want from each pillar in your next relationship. This is the beginning of your intentional living. Put your intention out into the universe by sharing it or at least saying it out loud. To manifest this intention, there are many steps you can take to improve your odds of Success.

1. Choose activities you enjoy and will likely share with a potential partner. Take a class to improve yourself, and you may meet someone on the same journey.

2. Engage in social activities that permit you to meet people in general, such as dancing, book clubs, travel, political organizing, and nonprofit volunteering.

3. Make friends first. You never know.

4. Become aware of expectations that arise and let go of them.

5. Talk to people you know about your intentions. They will help you on the path and reinforce the process. Discuss your Five Pillars with others. Make your intentions outwardly visible.

6. Modify the list as you make discoveries about yourself and others you meet.

7. Don't be in a hurry. Manifestation happens on the universe's time and not yours. Being patient with the universe's time yields extraordinary results.

THE ROLE OF EMPATHY

I had only considered the critical role of empathy in relationships once I learned from 23andMe in 2017 that genes are connected to one's ability to empathize. Some people have more genes for empathy than others, and women have specific genes that men do not have. Wow, that sure puts a new spin on relationships—and, of course, on human behavior in general.

However, for those who do not have an adequate supply of empathy genes, there is the ability to learn empathy. The discovery of the empathy gene led to the concept of emotional vs. cognitive empathy. Emotional empathy comes from the ability to sense or feel what someone else is feeling, while cognitive empathy is the identification of others' feelings through learned cues.

An example of cognitive empathy is when someone looks for facial cues to discern happiness or sadness. However, because the skill may not be well developed, they may mistake a pensive expression for anger or frustration.

Therefore, it is essential to understand how each party in a relationship is equipped to address the partner's emotions. If both parties are endowed with genetic and emotional sensibilities, it will likely be easy to know how the other is doing without saying a word.

Suppose one person in the relationship has good emotional empathy and the partner is not endowed or lacks cognitive empathy. In that case, there may be many moments of conflict caused by misunderstanding. But there is a solution.

Rick and Susan have a busy life raising three kids. He is a practicing attorney, and she is a physical therapist. They recently chose to go to couples counseling because they were constantly bickering. Rick feels he can't say the right thing no matter what he says. Susan thinks Rick ignores what is going on with her. After digging in a bit, they figure out that Rick doesn't have the empathy to understand where Susan is at. On the other hand, Susan is highly emotionally intuitive and knows how Rick feels by looking at or sensing his presence.

They figure out they can stop bickering if Rick stops, asks Susan how she is feeling and proceeds from what he hears. Susan agrees to stop reacting and to take time to let Rick know how she is feeling.

With both parties' willingness, symbolic emotional communication can be established. For example, if I rest my head in my hand, I feel tired. If I place my hand over my mouth, I don't feel like talking right now. Of course, we can also say how we feel.

Knowing this issue can help partners develop the skills needed to communicate feelings. If it is clear that your partner never knows when you have feelings of joy or sadness, you must express them verbally so they know.

Once a couple determines that communication has broken down due to an imbalance of empathy, it is helpful to rebuild the relationship on the foundation of the Five Pillars.

THE ROLE OF BOUNDARIES

The concept of boundaries is often lost in our culture. From the selfless love taught by some religions to society's self-entitled orientation, it isn't easy to understand what boundaries look like.

What is a boundary, anyway? It is simply a point in any human transaction indicating it is no longer feasible to carry out the transaction. An obvious example is telling my partner I will do anything for her. But if she asks me to kill someone for her, that is where that commitment stops. It is a clear boundary.

Boundaries are very much tied to values and are the existential embodiments of values in action. If I am committed to being a vegan, I may have a boundary that when served a dead animal to eat, I will not eat it.

Boundaries can be subtle, too. What is desirable by one partner in the bedroom may not be acceptable by the other. Boundaries include everything you will not say or do, regardless of your partner's influence.

Since boundaries connect to all our values, it is vital to ensure we are transparent about them in our relationships. Some may be negotiable, and some may not. But most importantly, boundaries should be discussed and not assumed. Communication, communication, communication.

Just as the Five Pillars are essential to building a positive connection in your relationship, understanding yours and your partner's boundaries is essential to Success.

COMMUNICATION

With good communication, any human transaction can stay strong. Communication is an essential tool for making the Five Pillars journey a successful one.

Sometimes, we get into a relationship where dysfunctional things start happening. Whether through communication, life getting in the way, or just little irritations, it may feel like it is time to end the relationship. We can consider talking about it, counseling, or giving up. However, in a long-term relationship, the solution sometimes appears more challenging than the problem.

The Two Major Components

We all learn to talk at a very early stage in life. We all know folks who are expert talkers. The party guy who holds court at every gathering, the professor who has no time for questions, and the spouse who tells you about their day but never asks about yours are all expert talkers.

Talking is not just making a statement about something. Do you have the listener's attention? Is there a context the listener should know? Is the message clear and concise? Are you using appropriate language? Are you being mindful when you speak? Is the timing right, or should you bite your tongue and wait, or say nothing?

Listening is often the component of communication that needs to be added or improved.

To have good communication, we need both talking and listening. But more precisely, we must actively listen—not just with our ears. What is the tone of voice and body language saying? What are the presenter's facial expressions, gestures, and posture?

And let's not forget the role of empathy. The speaker uses empathy to understand the listener and vice versa. Listening goes beyond the ears in many ways.

My partner and I agreed early in our relationship we would only start a discussion if we had permission from the other. We also decided not to ask questions or make statements from different rooms in the house. If we have something to say or a question to ask, we go to them first. Then, if the partner is busy doing something, we state that we have something to say or have a question "when you have a moment." The other person then has the opportunity to respond when ready to listen.

Feedback

Providing feedback verifies that the communication is complete, just like confirming an appointment. Saying what you heard slightly differently or rephrasing helps to clarify. But sometimes, a simple response is a nod of the head or a thumbs-up.

Barriers to Communication

It is common for humans to assume that every listener speaks the same language. But not everyone has the same education or has learned the same native language as you. You have heard the expression of someone saying, "It's like speaking to a child."

If you have raised kids, you get it. With every age of growth, the language becomes more sophisticated. Each child is different and raises your awareness of understanding your audience.

I was painfully reminded of understanding your audience when doing business overseas. Especially when doing business in Asia. Most Asian companies assume you do not speak their native language and have an English speaker on staff. But English is not their native language. Vocabulary had to be kept simple, and no complex sentences: subject, verb, object, and a period. Once I figured that out, there were far fewer misunderstandings.

One other barrier is what I call the stream-of-consciousness conversation. A friend will often assume I know what is going on in their lives at every moment and, without context, tell me the story about where they are currently at. I will have no idea what it all means without asking many questions. So, it reminds me I must provide the background or context to a conversation I start.

Dysfunctional Communication

The famous line from *Cool Hand Luke* brings the biggest problem of relationships to the fore:

"What we've got here is failure to communicate."

Bad habits, poor role models, cultural expectations, and selfish behavior are among the many influences of dysfunctional communication. Here are some of those habits:

- **Lack of Communication**: Failing to share thoughts, feelings, and concerns openly and honestly. Avoiding addressing important issues can lead to unresolved conflicts and increased tension. Stonewalling could also be classified as a lack of communication.

- **Suspicious Communication**: Exhibiting jealousy, suspicion, or paranoia that can erode the foundation of trust necessary for a stable relationship.
- **Manipulative Communication**: Using emotional manipulation to control or influence the other person's actions.
- **Critical Communication**: Frequently criticizing the partner, often focusing on their weaknesses or faults, which can lead to diminished self-esteem.
- **Dishonest Communication**: Dishonesty can destroy the trust essential to a healthy relationship.
- **Aggressive Communication**: Verbal aggression can create a toxic environment. Passive-aggressive communication is a more subtle form where the communication is indirectly aggressive.
- **Gaslighting Communication**: Manipulating someone into questioning their reality or sanity, typically to gain control.
- **Blaming Communication**: Consistently shifting responsibility and blame to the partner can prevent personal accountability and growth.

The good news is we can change communication and work toward healthy relationships. Sometimes, this can be easily worked out between two mature adults. If you fail, it is time to get third-party help. If the Five Pillars are strong, you increase your chances for Success.

DYSFUNCTIONAL BEHAVIOR

It seems idyllic when we have all these fantastic ideas to build a great relationship, but what if one or both parties engage in dysfunctional behavior? What happens?

Unshared Values

Any behavior that does not support the shared values of the partners in a relationship is dysfunctional for all intents and purposes. So, what may be dysfunctional in one relationship may not be so in another. For example, if monogamy is highly valued and one partner is frequently having affairs, the resulting infidelity is dysfunctional. However, if the shared value is to have an open relationship, the behavior would not be dysfunctional.

Another example is the drinking of alcohol. If both members value drinking as a part of the relationship, it can be a very functional activity. If one of the members of the relationship is opposed to drinking alcohol, it could create a dysfunctional situation. But again, this is a relative situation. If the non-drinking partner is supportive of the behavior of the drinking partner, it may be a perfectly functional situation.

And then, of course, there is the issue of addiction and alcoholism. Many folks go into relationships without knowing the existence of the problem. These issues are more related to personality or mental disorders and require different attention than dysfunctional behavior.

Dysfunctional behavior can also be habits that are not to the liking of one of the partners. It is dysfunctional because it makes the relationship more stressful. However, because habits can be traced back to value breakdowns, a discussion of the shared values may call attention to the behavior contrary to the value. For example, Susan gets irritated with Bob because he always leaves his dirty clothes on the floor in the bedroom. She finally confronts him and asks him why he does it. They share the value of a clean and tidy house, but this behavior is not that. After a short discussion, they realize it all started when the laundry basket broke. Bob's habit of putting them in the laundry basket was interrupted, and he never had time to think it through. They decide to purchase a new one, and the problem is solved.

Solving dysfunctional behavior is not a problem with two mature adults. The issues can be talked through. Once identified, assuming willingness, the behavior is stopped, or the person with the dysfunction gets help to change it. The more closely aligned the Five Pillars are, the quicker the behavior can be resolved.

PERSONALITY DISORDERS

I had a friend who was dealing with a horrible marriage. Her husband was both verbally and physically abusive. I tried to talk her into walking away, but she felt her religious commitments did not support that solution. Eventually, she talked her husband into visiting a professional counselor within their religious denomination. After a few days of therapy, the therapist took her aside and told her that her husband had a personality disorder. At the rate the violence had escalated, she felt it best to leave as soon as possible. She drove home, packed up, and left.

While some dysfunctional behavior may be modified with cognitive behavioral therapy (CBT) and other techniques, personality disorders are generally more difficult, if not impossible, to change. Mild personality disorders may be manageable with the right help, but they are also challenging to diagnose. CBT is a form of psychotherapy that focuses on identifying and changing negative thought patterns and behaviors. It is based on the concept that our thoughts, feelings, and behaviors are interconnected and that changing negative thoughts and maladaptive behaviors can lead to changes in feelings and overall mental well-being.

Personality disorders include paranoid, schizoid, antisocial, borderline, histrionic, narcissistic, avoidant, dependent, and obsessive-compulsive. There are many good resources to dig deeper into personality disorders. Contact a local psychologist or psychiatrist or look online for mental health services. Get help.

FOR BETTER OR WORSE

For many in our culture, marriage is a symbol of commitment. Religiously, it suggests commitment until death. However, there are many ways it can begin to fail. It could be realizing different values or goals, not having any activities in common, or just not knowing what you want to give or get. It could be irreconcilable differences, dysfunctional behavior, or just dysfunctional communication.

Review the Five Pillars

Before you give up on a relationship or start counseling, it is time to review the Five Pillars and how they relate to you. Both parties should take a piece of paper and review the book's list of values, goals, and activities (*see Table of Contents*). List your top five in each group. Then, discuss these and see if there is enough in common to build upon.

After the values, goals, and activities have been discussed, you can move on to the two big questions that are often not discussed:

> What do I want to give to this relationship?
> What do I want to get from this relationship?

Finding the intersection of these two questions after a discussion will give you both an idea of whether there is a direction to continue. At the very least, if the answers are ambiguous or poorly articulated, you can take what you have to your relationship counselor.

Hitting the Reset Button

After reviewing the Five Pillars, you and your partner may decide to "start over." In essence, hit the reset button of your relationship. You may have discovered more to your relationship than you anticipated during your review of the Five Pillars.

First, solidify your commitment to your shared values. With common values, there is more to go forward with.

Second, write down your one-year and five-year goals together and individually. Once we know our partners' goals, we can help them reach their goals as they help us reach our goals. And, of course, how you both will serve to achieve your mutual goals.

Third, figure out what activities you like to do together. Things may have changed as you have grown older together. For example, you both may have aged out of mountain biking, but a bike ride to the local park and back is very doable. But crossover activities work also. Randy and Jeanie used to ski together. Jeanie has an injury and no longer enjoys it but loves going to the resorts. So, she takes a book to read and meets up with Randy for lunch or a drink during the day.

When to Quit

Sometimes, there is just no way to make the relationship work. It is probably not salvageable when you discover you and your partner have no values in common. When goals are so far apart that one person will move to the other side of the planet and the other will not, it may be time to quit. When activities are so divergent that nothing seems possible together, it is time to move on. And if the giving-and-getting equation of the relationship has no redemption, it is most likely time to quit.

But before quitting, take the information you have gathered and find a reputable third party you both trust to help you. Whether it is a couples counselor, therapy group, religious leader, or other trained intermediary, trying to find a solution to working with your partner is time well spent. At worst, you will have more insight into how you can do better in your subsequent relationships.

WRAPPING IT UP

Relationships are not simple, but they can be wonderful. They can provide partnerships that last a lifetime. Whether you are in one now or starting a new one, the Five Pillars can provide a foundation for you to build on what you have, solve some problems that may have evolved, or be the basis for starting a new one.

I applied the philosophy to my own life and have had a blissful and successful relationship ever since. It has also helped me deepen friendships and avoid getting involved with people I have no business befriending.

If the process seems overwhelming, start with a few simple steps.

1. Write down your most important values, goals, and activities. Describe at least a couple of things you want to give and things you want to get in a relationship.
2. Ask your partner or potential partner if they want to discuss them.

3. Find common ground in each aspect of the Five Pillars.

Hopefully, this will all lead to a meaningful conversation and a deeper connection. Best wishes on your relationship journey.

ABOUT THE AUTHOR

Lester Karplus graduated from the University of Illinois with Distinction, majoring in Philosophy and Community Psychology. He spent a couple of years working in mental health before moving on to working in natural foods. He has spent most of his life as an entrepreneur in natural food, software, and electronics and has written many technical books. He retired to Panama with his wife, Karna, and entered a new chapter of his life, writing stories and practical insights into living.